WEIRD SEA CREATURES™

THE SEA DRAGON

Miriam J. Gross

The Rosen Publishing Group's
PowerKids Press™
New York

For Corinna

Published in 2006 by The Rosen Publishing Group, Inc.
29 East 21st Street, New York, NY 10010

First Edition

Editor: Daryl Heller
Book Design: Albert B. Hanner
Layout Design: Greg Tucker

Photo Credits: Cover, p. 5 © James D. Watt/SeaPics.com; p. 6 © Paul A. Sutherland/SeaPics.com; p. 9 © Darryl Torckler/Getty Images; p. 10 © Michael Aw/SeaPics.com; p. 13 © Tim Rock/SeaPics.com; pp. 14, 18, 21 © John C. Lewis/SeaPics.com; p. 17 © Doug Perrine/SeaPics.com.

Library of Congress Cataloging-in-Publication Data

Gross, Miriam J.
The sea dragon / Miriam J. Gross.
p. cm. — (Weird sea creatures)
Includes index.
ISBN 1-4042-3193-5 (lib. bdg.)
1. Leafy seadragon—Juvenile literature. 2. Weedy seadragon—Juvenile literature. I. Title.

QL638.S9G74 2006
597'.679—dc22
                        2005001477

Manufactured in Malaysia

CONTENTS

A Floating Dragon

A sea dragon is almost impossible to find when it swims among the underwater plants where it lives. This small creature looks like a piece of floating seaweed or sea grass that grows on the ocean floor. However, when this animal is viewed alone it looks like a floating dragon.

Sea dragons get their name from the bits of flesh that cover their bodies, which look almost like a dragon's wings. These creatures swim slowly, swaying back and forth and up and down. This movement looks like plants drifting in the water currents. Sea dragons are brightly colored and striped. They have large, dark eyes.

These strange creatures are beautiful and unusual. Sea dragons are so delicate, or easily hurt, that they can only be found in one place in the world. They live in the **shallow** coastal waters off the **continent** of Australia. By learning more about sea dragons, we may be able to save these animals before they disappear.

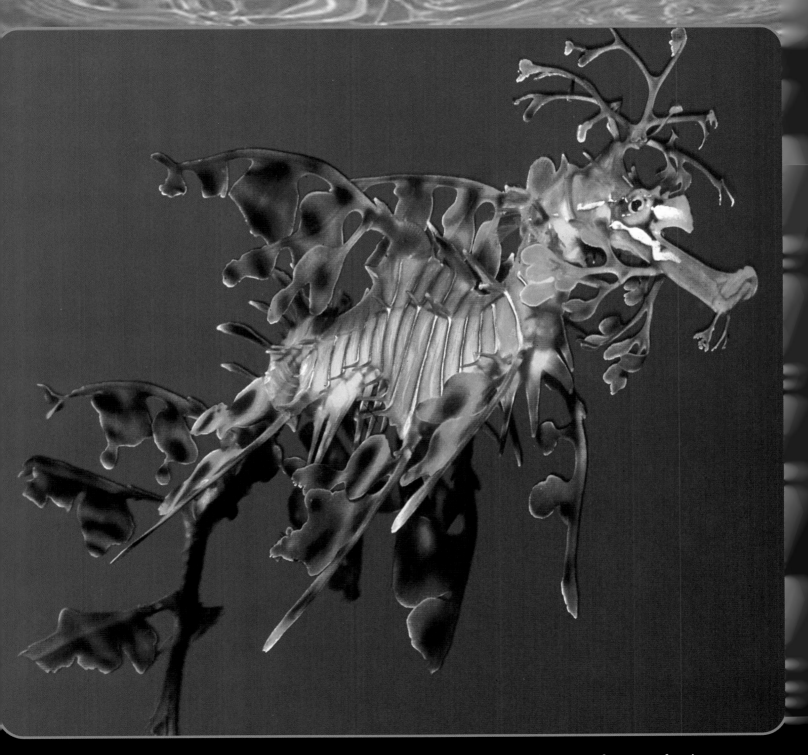

This leafy sea dragon swims off the coast of Kangaroo Island in Australia. The scientific name for the leafy sea dragon is Phycodurus eques. Kangaroo Island is the third largest island in Australia.

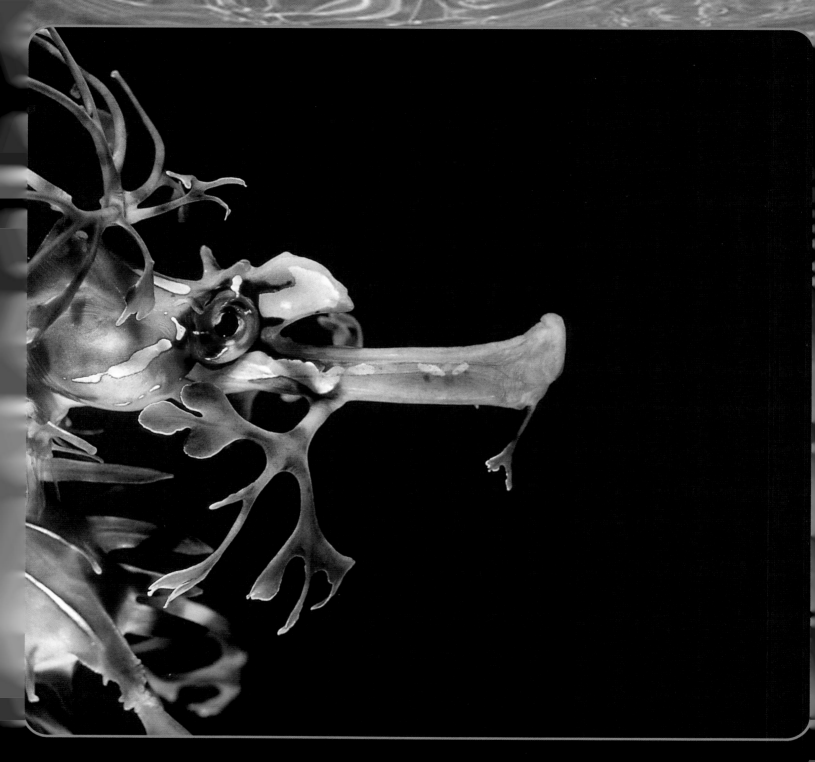

This is a close-up of the head of a leafy sea dragon. The creature's long snout has a mouth on the end tha[

MEET THE FAMILY

Although sea dragons look like fairy-tale dragons, they are actually a type of fish. Like all fish they have gills, which are **organs** that take in oxygen from the water. Oxygen is a gas that animals need to live. They also have a **backbone**, as do all other fish.

Sea dragons are related to sea horses and pipefishes. They are all part of a group of fish that scientists call Syngnathidae. *Syngnathidae* means "**fused jaws**" in Greek. The animals got this name because of their **snout**. This snout is long and tube shaped, with a small, toothless mouth on the end. Because the snout does not open or close it is considered fused. Members of the Syngnathidae family also have an external skeleton. This is a hard covering around the outside of their body that **protects** the creatures and gives them their shape.

One unusual thing about fish in the Syngnathidae family is that the fathers carry the eggs. Each male has a special area on his body where he keeps the eggs safe and warm while they grow. Later the babies will break free from the father.

WEEDY AND LEAFY

The leafy sea dragon lives in water from 30 to 90 feet (9 to 27 m) below the surface. The weedy sea dragon lives farther down at about 165 feet (50 m) below the surface. The coloring of each species matches the plant life found at these different depths. However, sea dragons can sometimes change color slightly, depending on the food they eat, their age, and what happens around them.

There are two **species** of sea dragons. The weedy sea dragon is the most common. This creature has a reddish orange body with yellow spots on its back and blue stripes along its belly. Its snout is long and thin, and it has a long tail. Small **appendages** that look like bits of seaweed stick out from this sea dragon's head, body, and tail. The appendages help the sea dragon match the seaweed that surrounds it. Weedy sea dragons can grow to 18 inches (46 cm) long.

The leafy sea dragon is the other species. Branching, leaf-shaped appendages surround its body and tail. The leafy sea dragon can be green or yellowish brown, with dark pink stripes across its body. The snout is slightly wider than the weedy sea dragon's, and sharp spines, or thorns, protect the sides of its body. Leafy sea dragons are usually about 12 inches (30 cm) long.

This is a pair of leafy sea dragons. Like most other fish, sea dragons have a swim bladder. The swim bladder is a pocket of gas inside the fish that allows the fish to control its depth, or how far down it swims in the water. This keeps the fish from sinking to the bottom of the ocean or floating up to the surface.

Other fish might easily miss these two leafy sea dragons. The sea dragons are camouflaged because they

HIDING IN PLAIN SIGHT

The sea dragon's plantlike appendages make it almost impossible to see this animal among the seaweed in which it lives. When creatures are able to match their surroundings in this way, scientists say they are camouflaged. The creature even sways from side to side like a piece of seaweed. The sea dragon's perfect **mimicry** of a plant keeps it hidden from predators. A predator is an animal that hunts and kills other animals for food.

Both species of sea dragon have hard external skeletons. Leafy sea dragons also have long, sharp spines on their sides that can help prevent attacks from hungry fish.

While adult sea dragons have no known natural predators, the young have a harder time. At birth they do not have all the appendages it takes to mimic plants. Fish, **crustaceans**, and sea urchins all **prey** on the tiny young sea dragons.

A Suit of Armor

A sea dragon has a **hide** of hard, bony rings that covers its body. The hide protects the sea dragon like a suit of **armor** worn by a knight. However, it also makes it hard for the creature to move around. Most other fish use their flexible, or bendable, tail fins to push them through the water. The sea dragon's body is so stiff that it can only move by **oscillating** its tiny ventral and dorsal fins. The ventral fins are set near the sides of the creature's head. The dorsal fins are on the creature's back. Since it is not a good swimmer, a sea dragon spends most of its time slowly floating among seaweed.

The sea dragon has two large eyes that can move separately from each other. Because one eye can look up while the other eye looks down, the sea dragon can see all around itself. This helps the creature find food and avoid danger from either above or below.

The bony pointed growths that stick out from this creature's body are called the hide. The scientific

mysid

This two-week-old weedy sea dragon floats near some of its favorite prey, mysid shrimp. The weedy sea

EATING

The sea dragon feeds on **plankton**, baby fish, and especially a species of tiny shrimp called mysids. Mysids belong to the scientific group of animals known as crustaceans. The sea dragon has no teeth. This creature uses its long snout to draw prey and water into its mouth.

The sea dragon hunts by pretending to be seaweed. As mysids or other prey approach what they think is just a floating plant, the sea dragon opens a joint on the lower part of its snout. This causes a suction force, like sucking through a straw, and the prey is drawn in through the sea dragon's mouth.

Because the creatures that the sea dragon eats are so small, the sea dragon must spend a lot of its time eating. This hungry little fish may spend as long as 10 hours eating up to 3,000 mysids or other prey in a single day.

UNDERWATER GARDENS

Water pressure is the force created by the weight of water. Water pressure is greater the deeper down you go. This is because there is more water pushing down on you. Gas is lighter than water. The gas inside a fish's swim bladder helps a fish from being weighed down by water pressure.

The weedy sea dragon and the leafy sea dragon can only be found on the coast of southern Australia. This area's seaweed, clean water, and **mild** weather make it the perfect **habitat** for such delicate creatures. Both species live among beds of seaweed, **coral reefs**, and meadows of sea grass, a grass that grows in salt water. A sea dragon floats near the sandy ocean floor not far from the coast. This creature is **sensitive** to changes in water pressure and may die if the water pressure changes too quickly.

The sea dragon needs its special habitat to stay alive. Today, however, litter often **pollutes** the sea grass meadows and seaweed beds. **Fertilizer** runoff can also make the water poisonous. The runoff occurs when people use too much fertilizer in their yards. When it rains the rainwater carries the extra fertilizer into streams that end up in the ocean.

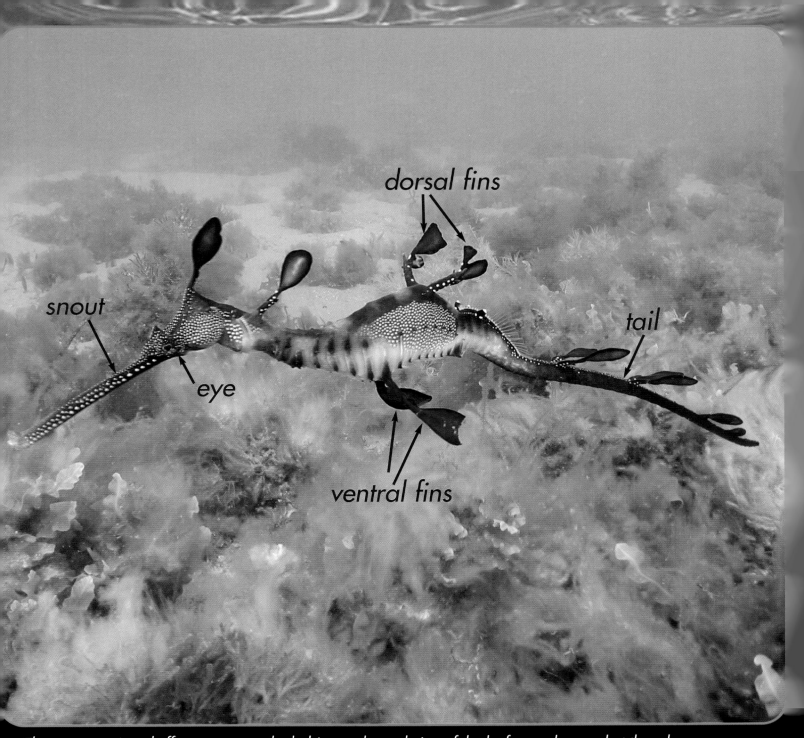

dorsal fins

snout

eye

tail

ventral fins

There are continued efforts to protect the habitat and population of the leafy sea dragon, but there have been fewer attempts to protect the weedy sea dragon, which is shown above. This is because there are more weedy sea dragons than there are leafy sea dragons. Leafy sea dragons are also more likely to be

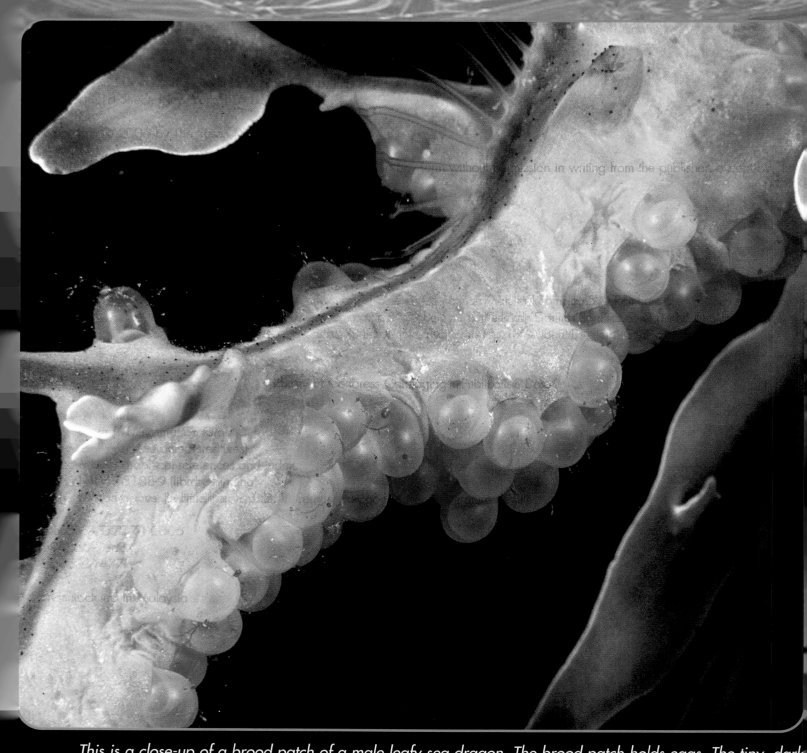

This is a close-up of a brood patch of a male leafy sea dragon. The brood patch holds eggs. The tiny, dark eyes of the baby sea dragons can be seen inside the eggs. The brood patch is on the underside, or

MATING

When spring warms the waters of Australia's southern coast, sea dragons pair off to **mate**. When the female is ready to mate, her abdomen, or belly, swells with eggs. The male's tail increases in size and wrinkles. The male swims close to the female. The male and female will spend about one day floating up and down in the water together.

Like all members of the Syngnathidae family, it is the male sea dragon that bears children. He has a special place under his tail called the brood patch. The brood patch is made up of cups of **tissue** that hold the eggs. The female drops her bright pink eggs in the male's brood patch, where the male **fertilizes** them. Tissue then grows around the eggs to protect them. The male **incubates** the eggs under his tail for four to six weeks.

The sea dragon's breeding season lasts from August to March. In Australia spring begins in August. The female can lay from 100 to 250 eggs at a time. The male usually hatches two batches of eggs every season.

LIFE CYCLE

Baby sea dragons hatch just a few at a time. This gives each one a better chance of finding food without having to compete, or struggle, with its brothers and sisters. A litter of 200 eggs may take 10 days to hatch.

Sea dragons are only about 0.8 inches (20 mm) long when they are born. They look just like adult sea dragons, except that they are black and silver in color and have fewer plantlike appendages.

As soon as the babies leave their father's brood patch, these creatures must take care of themselves. Large fish eat many of the young sea dragons.

After a few weeks, the young sea dragons begin to change color. Weedy sea dragons take on the red or brown shades of adults. Leafy sea dragons turn shades of yellow and green. In the first year, the young sea dragons can grow to be about 8 inches (20 cm) long.

At about two years of age, sea dragons are fully grown and ready to mate. Sea dragons usually live about five to seven years. They often live alone but are sometimes found in groups or pairs.

This is a leafy sea dragon at around one week old. Parents of sea dragons do not care for their young

DRAGONS IN DANGER

In some sea grass beds in Australia, sea dragons have already disappeared. They are hurt when sea grass meadows and seaweed beds become polluted. Sea dragons can also be harmed by bad weather. A storm can upset the balance of water pressure that sea dragons require and piles of them may wash up on beaches. Many sea dragons were once caught for use in Asian medicines, or drugs. Others were caught and sold as pets. Divers trying to shoot pictures of sea dragons can scare the creatures enough to cause them harm.

The Australian government is trying to protect these creatures. Sea dragons cannot be hunted or taken from Australia without a special government permit. Aquariums such as the Aquarium of Western Australia are also trying to raise sea dragons in tanks. This will help scientists learn more about the sea dragon's life cycle. These studies will also allow scientists to return healthy sea dragon babies to the wild and increase their population. Sea dragons have a better chance of remaining on our planet if we protect them and their habitats.

GLOSSARY

appendages (uh-PEN-dij-ez) Parts of a living thing that stick out from the body.

armor (AR-mer) A type of uniform often made of metal that keeps the body from harm.

backbone (BAK-bohn) A set of bones in an animal's back that gives the animal shape.

continent (KON-teh-nent) One of Earth's seven large landmasses.

coral reefs (KOR-ul REEFS) Underwater hills of coral. Coral is hard matter made up of the bones of tiny sea animals.

crustaceans (krus-TAY-shunz) Animals that have no backbone and have a hard shell and limbs.

fertilizer (FUR-tuh-lyz-er) Matter put in soil to help crops grow.

fertilizes (FUR-tuh-lyz-ez) Puts male cells inside female's eggs to make babies.

fused (FYOOZD) Joined together.

habitat (HA-bih-tat) The surroundings where an animal or a plant naturally lives.

hide (HYD) The skin of an animal.

incubates (IN-kyoo-bayts) Keeps eggs warm, usually at body temperature.

jaws (JAHZ) Part of the mouths of many animals.

mate (MAYT) To join together to make babies.

mild (MYLD) Warm and without much change.

mimicry (MIH-mik-ree) Copying something else closely to look like it.

organs (OR-genz) Parts inside the body that do a job.

oscillating (AH-seh-layt-ing) Moving back and forth at a regular speed.

plankton (PLANK-ten) Plants and animals that drift with water currents.

pollutes (puh-LOOTS) Poisons with harmful matter.

prey (PRAY) To hunt for food.

protects (pruh-TEKTS) Keeps from harm.

sensitive (SEN-sih-tiv) Able to see or feel small differences.

shallow (SHA-loh) Not deep.

snout (SNOWT) The long nose of an animal such as a pig or a horse.

species (SPEE-sheez) A single kind of living thing. All people are one species.

tissue (TIH-shoo) Matter that forms the parts of living things.

INDEX

WEB SITES

Due to the changing nature of Internet links, PowerKids Press has developed an online list of Web sites related to the subject of this book. This site is updated regularly. Please use this link to access the list:

www.powerkidslinks.com/wsc/seadragon/